The Upstairs Cuckoo

A farce

Peter Horsler

Samuel French—London
New York—Hollywood—Toronto

Copyright © 1992 by Samuel French Ltd
All Rights Reserved

THE UPSTAIRS CUCKOO is fully protected under the copyright laws of the British Commonwealth, including Canada, the United States of America, and all other countries of the Copyright Union. All rights, including professional and amateur stage productions, recitation, lecturing, public reading, motion picture, radio broadcasting, television and the rights of translation into foreign languages are strictly reserved.

ISBN 978-0-573-12283-5

www.samuelfrench.co.uk
www.samuelfrench.com

FOR AMATEUR PRODUCTION ENQUIRIES

UNITED KINGDOM AND WORLD
EXCLUDING NORTH AMERICA
plays@samuelfrench.co.uk
020 7255 4302/01

Each title is subject to availability from Samuel French, depending upon country of performance.

CAUTION: Professional and amateur producers are hereby warned that THE UPSTAIRS CUCKOO is subject to a licensing fee. Publication of this play does not imply availability for performance. Both amateurs and professionals considering a production are strongly advised to apply to the appropriate agent before starting rehearsals, advertising, or booking a theatre. A licensing fee must be paid whether the title is presented for charity or gain and whether or not admission is charged.

The professional rights in this play are controlled by Samuel French Ltd, 24-32 Stephenson Way, London, NW1 2HD.

No one shall make any changes in this title for the purpose of production. No part of this book may be reproduced, stored in a retrieval system, or transmitted in any form, by any means, now known or yet to be invented, including mechanical, electronic, photocopying, recording, videotaping, or otherwise, without the prior written permission of the publisher. No one shall upload this title, or part of this title, to any social media websites.

The right of Peter Horsler to be identified as author of this work has been asserted in accordance with Section 77 of the Copyright, Designs and Patents Act 1988.

CHARACTERS

Claire
Derek, Claire's live-in boyfriend
Libby, Claire's daughter
Steve, Claire's estranged husband

THE UPSTAIRS CUCKOO

The kitchen-diner of a small semi in suburbia

A small hallway can be seen UR which is on a slightly higher level than the rest of the acting area. The raised area leads off R to the front door which is not visible and to the L the foot of the stairway can just be seen. There is a table UC of this area on which stands a telephone. Below this hallway is the main acting area where there is a small coffee table set DR with two easy-type chairs above it and a small dining-table, on which is a folded cloth, set L. Three chairs are placed against the L wall. An entrance UL leads to the kitchen

When the CURTAIN *rises, Claire is on the phone*

Claire (*on the phone*) Yes, yes, all right, Libby, but there is a difference. Yes, I know I've left Daddy and am living with Derek but that's not the same as you shacking up with Tony. ... Why not? Well, I'm a married woman to start with. ... All right, I might not be married to the man I'm living with but —— Yes, well, when you have a daughter you'll understand. ... Let's change the subject, shall we. Did you remember to place that advert for me? ... Which advert? There was only one. I've never asked you to put an advert in a paper before, have I? ... I did. When you came round last week.

There is the sound of the front door opening and shutting

Derek enters UR

Well, I know I did.
Derek (*passing Claire, glancing at her*) Not ringing hubby, I hope. You promised never to speak to him again, remember.
Claire Just a minute, love.
Derek My word, absence does make the heart grow fonder.
Claire (*covering the mouthpiece*) It's Libby, idiot.
Derek (*coming to sit in the easy-chair* DR) I hope she can't hear that, calling your daughter an idiot. It's not nice.
Claire (*on the phone*) It's only Derek.
Derek Only.
Claire (*on the phone*) So you haven't ...? You have. Oh, you idiot!
Derek You're doing it again.
Claire (*on the phone*) Having me on like that. So you did. When? ... Good, that would have been in last night's paper.
Derek What would have?
Claire (*to Derek*) Never mind. (*On the phone*) No, I was talking to Derek. All right, love, see you later, perhaps. (*She puts the phone down, comes down and puts her arms round Derek's neck*) You knew that was Libby. You know I would never call Steve "love". Not any more. He's — he's a ... well, he's a man!
Derek Thanks very much. Have you seen my handbag?
Claire (*sitting on his* L) No, I mean he's a man by my mother's definition.
Derek (*with understanding*) Ah.
Claire You're my idea of a man: dependable, gentle, considerate ——
Derek Dull.
Claire No: warm, loving, cuddly.
Derek Old.
Claire Only a bit older than me. A woman likes her man to be a

The Upstairs Cuckoo

little older, more experienced, serene. That swine Steve is over a year younger than me.

Derek He's no gentleman. A gentleman always arranges to be born before a woman.

Claire Like a drink?

Derek Thanks, it has been a gruelling day.

Claire (*going off* UL) I think there's some cooking sherry left over from Christmas.

Claire exits

Derek (*calling to her*) Cooking sherry! That's just what a man needs after a hard day's work. Haven't you seen all the adverts? "If you're feeling crook, get cracking with the cooking sherry!" Notice it doesn't say what you're to do with it.

Claire enters carrying a sherry bottle and two glasses. She sets the glasses down on the small coffee-table and fills them from the bottle

Claire You wouldn't catch me talking to that swine. He'll give me a trouble-free divorce if I have to kill him for it.

Derek I don't think they do posthumous divorce.

Claire There he is raking in huge profits and we're struggling in poverty.

Derek On about £35,000 actually, with our combined salaries.

Claire Twenty of it goes to Camilla to pay off her debts.

Derek Only temporarily. She's torn up her credit cards.

Claire (*giving him his sherry and sitting on his* L) You're divorced from her, Derek, for goodness sake. You don't have to pay any more than the court settlement. I can't imagine Steve giving me my just dues never mind about a bit extra.

Derek I don't want him giving you anything extra. I don't want

to hear another word about Steve. He doesn't interest me; he's the past, I'm the present.
Claire (*moving to the table and putting a cloth on it*) And never the twain shall meet.
Derek Right.
Claire You're not even curious about him, are you? (*She places two chairs L and R of the table*)
Derek If I don't know anything about him, I can imagine him just as I like. In my book he's got a hump back, bloodshot, piggy eyes, a club foot, a slobbery, loose mouth and horns on his head.
Claire So you do know him.
Derek Steve and Camilla are taboo from now on, right?
Claire (*coming back to sit on his L*) Right, not another word.

Long pause

Derek Any post today?
Claire No. (*Long pause*) Have a good day?
Derek No.

Long pause

Claire Did you get to the bank?
Derek Yes.
Claire Good.
Derek Not good.
Claire Oh.
Derek The cupboard was bare.
Claire I see. (*Pause*) Well, I've got a good idea to solve our immediate financial problems.
Derek Oh.
Claire Yes, let the spare bedroom.
Derek Let the ... ? You mean take a lodger?

Claire Why not?
Derek You want a stranger in our little heaven?
Claire Well, it would help to solve a problem.
Derek And create others. She might mess up your kitchen.
Claire *He* wouldn't go near my kitchen.
Derek He might get drunk; bring other women here.
Claire All right, forget it. We'll manage somehow.
Derek No, it's worth considering.
Claire Well, after all you've — isn't that typical.
Derek In fact, I've already put an advert in this week's paper.
Claire (*jumping up*) You've done what?
Derek We discussed it.
Claire We damned well didn't!
Derek You think it's a good idea though?
Claire I think it's a lousy idea!
Derek We can always say no.
Claire "We"! You do mean "We"? (*Moving* DL *arms folded, facing out front*) You're no better than he is. If you think I'm putting up with being a rubber stamp with you as well, you've got another think coming!
Derek (*jumping up and moving to her*) All right, all right. I'm sorry. It's just that Camilla always left all the business to me. I thought I'd asked your opinion.
Claire (*pushing him away and moving to exit* UR) Liar! And you can answer all the phone calls, turn away all the callers and do the washing up!

She sweeps off and then returns for a parting shot

Derek has moved to follow her but jumps back as she returns

I'm off then. I haven't made up my mind whether to pop next door for some herbs or enter a nunnery. Give any would-be lodgers a flea in the ear for me, would you?

She goes off UR

The front door slams

Derek sighs, empties his sherry back into the bottle and takes it and the two glasses off UL *to the kitchen*

The phone rings

Derek enters

Derek (*answering the phone*) Hallo. ... Yes, you've got the right number but I'm afraid there's had to be a change of plan, the room's no longer available. ... No, unforseen circumstances. ... Yes, sorry. (*He puts the phone down*)

The front doorbell rings

Derek exits UR *to answer it*

(*Off*) Yes?
Steve (*off*) Good-evening, I believe you advertised a room.
Derek (*off*) Er, yes, but ——
Steve (*off*) Not taken, is it?
Derek (*off*) Er no, but ——
Steve (*off*) Mind if I take a look?

Steve enters

The front door closes

Derek follows Steve in

Derek Er, you'd better come in.

The Upstairs Cuckoo

Steve Thanks. (*Taking his hand*) The name's Steve, by the way. A young friend suggested that I look in this area.
Derek Look, er — Steve, I'll show you the room but I can't give you a decision today. Domestic crisis, you know.
Steve Really?
Derek Yes, minor problems. Can let you know in a couple of days. (*Leading the way upstairs*) Anyway, better see if it's what you want first, hadn't we?
Steve (*following*) Yes. I know precisely what I want.

They disappear upstairs. There is the sound of a key in the front door and the door opens and closes. Claire enters

Claire Derek? (*Going to the kitchen*) Derek, can you come?

Claire goes into the kitchen. Derek comes hastily downstairs

Derek Shush!

Claire enters

Claire What?
Derek Not so loud. You'll, er, you'll disturb the neighbours.
Claire What are you on about? Zoe's not worried about noise. In fact she'd love some right now. She can't get her car to start again. Can you come?
Derek (*taking a quick glance upstairs*) It's not terribly convenient. I'm afraid ——
Claire Oh come on, Zoe's good enough to lend us some herbs for dinner tonight. It's the least ——
Derek All right, I'll take a quick look.

Derek goes off UR. *Claire follows him off and there is the sound of the door closing. Libby enters* UL

Libby Mum, that back door is sticking again —— (*Realizing she's not there and looking off* UR) Mum?

Steve comes downstairs

Libby comes back to see him at the foot of the stairs

Dad!
Steve (*holding his finger to his lip*) Don't make a sound.
Libby What?
Steve It's an experiment.

He takes her arm and leads her downstage

Libby What is?
Steve I'm going to become the lodger.
Libby But you can't. Derek won't allow it and Mum will go mad.
Steve Derek doesn't know me from Adam and I think I can handle your mother.
Libby Oh yes? Well, you've made a great success of that in the past, haven't you?
Steve Well, it was your idea. Why else would you let me know she was going to take a lodger?
Libby I wanted you to know how hard up she was. I thought you might want to help her out.
Steve You surely don't expect me to finance her adultery, do you?
Libby Just what are you up to?
Steve Don't you want us to get back together?
Libby (*slumping into the* R *armchair*) Not if it's going to be like it was before. You were demoralizing Mum, do you know that? Reducing her to a cipher.
Steve Nonsense. (*Moving to her*) She liked me to take the initiative. She can't stand weak men.

Libby She'll make Derek throw you out.
Steve (*breaking away*) Him? He couldn't throw the cat out.
Libby Well, we'll see, won't we.

Derek enters

Derek Sorry about that. (*Seeing Libby*) Oh, Libby. (*To Steve*) I see you've met my daughter.
Libby Well, I'm not actually ——
Steve Oh, really.
Derek Only by adoption.
Steve (*moving to Libby, leaning over her*) Adopted are you?
Derek Unofficially, just by mutual consent.
Libby You see, my father deserted me.
Steve How awful for you. You must miss him terribly.
Derek Best thing that ever happened to her. He was an absolute swine.
Steve Knew him well, I suppose?
Derek Oh yes. Didn't have a saving grace.
Libby Mummy could never have him back.
Steve Wouldn't be too sure, if I were you.
Derek I beg your pardon?
Steve I couldn't be more sure.
Derek What?
Steve About the room. I just love it.
Derek Oh, the room! Of course. But I shall have to square it with Claire, my wife, you know.
Steve No, I didn't know.
Derek Course not. Why should you.
Libby Why indeed? Anyway, Mummy won't mind about us having a lodger will she? I mean, she was the one who put the advert in the paper.
Derek 'Fraid not.
Libby But she did. She got me to do it for her.

Derek Did she? Well, that must make it all right then. Steve — it is Steve isn't it? — the room is yours.
Steve (*shaking his hand*) Thanks, old man, you'll never regret it.
Libby (*getting up and moving to the kitchen*) Wouldn't be too sure, if I were you.
Derek Really, Libby, that is a bit uncalled for.

Libby stops and turns

Libby Sorry. I can't think what made me say that.
Steve No offence taken.
Libby I'm so pleased. Well, I'm off, Derek. See you.

Libby goes into the kitchen

Steve Aren't you going to wait to see your mother?

Libby pops back

Libby Can't just now. Not a good time. See you.

Libby exits through the kitchen

Derek Sorry. She's normally very polite.
Steve Just a little flustered. Kids are like that with strangers. I say, I don't want to be the cause of any friction between you and your wife.
Derek She's not actually.
Steve Not your wife?
Derek I think it better you know. It doesn't worry you that we're not married, does it?
Steve Not a bit.
Derek Good. Well, when would you like to move in?

Steve At once. If that's all right. I've got all I need in the car.
Derek Oh, well, it will be a bit of a shock to Claire — but it was her idea.
Steve She'll get over it. I mean, women are very adaptable, aren't they?
Derek Right. I'll give you a hand. You'll have to settle the details with her — as it was her idea.
Steve Right. I'm looking forward to meeting her. I only hope she takes to me.
Derek (*ushering Steve towards the front door*) Oh, I'm sure she will. Marvellous judge of character. She'll recognize your worth directly she sees you.

They exit UR

Libby (*off* UL, *distant*) Mum! Mum!

Claire enters UL

Claire Derek? (*She discovers the room is empty*)

Libby follows her in

Libby Mum, I tried to catch you. (*Realizing that Derek and Steve are not there*) Oh!
Claire I was only next door.
Libby I know, I saw you come out.
Claire What's all the panic about?
Libby It's Dad.
Claire (*gathering up the glasses*) I see. Nothing important then.
Libby Would you have him back?
Claire Don't start all that again, Libby. Nothing would induce me to stay under the same roof as that man ever again. So there

is absolutely no point in you pleading his case — and I've got to get our dinner on the table — (*moving* UL) — so if that's all you came for ...

Claire exits UL

Libby (*following her*) It's no good you carrying on, Mum, I know how you feel.

Libby exits. Derek enters UR *carrying a large case. Steve follows him, carrying a much smaller one. Derek puts his down in the hall to take a breather*

Derek Hell, that's heavy. What on earth have you got in it, bricks?
Steve Books, for my wife.
Derek I say, you're not bringing her, are you?
Steve No, no need, you see.
Derek Eh?
Steve We don't live together any more.
Derek Oh, that's a relief.
Steve What?
Derek I mean that she's not coming. There's only a single bed in that room.
Steve Yes, pity.
Derek Yes, sorry.
Steve Better get unpacked then.
Derek (*picking up the case and moving up the stairs*) Right.

Steve follows him and they disappear upstairs. Claire enters UL

Claire (*looking around and then calling to the kitchen*) No, your handbag's not here.

The Upstairs Cuckoo

Libby enters UL

Libby It's all right, I've just remembered, I didn't bring it.
Claire Well done. At least this time we didn't call out the National Guard. Dinner's ready if you want to stay. There's plenty for three.
Libby Can't, can I? I've got Thingy's meal to get.
Claire "Thingy"? How romantic. I just love the pet names you two call each other.
Libby Oh? What does he call me then?
Claire Never mind, it's better you don't know.

Derek enters down the stairs

(*To Derek*) Oh, there you are. I didn't hear you come in. Did you fix Zoe's car?
Derek Well you should know: you stayed talking to her for ages with the engine running.
Claire Was it? I didn't notice.

Libby starts a dumb show with Derek

Libby (*pointing up, mouthing silently*) Is he up there?
Claire You all right, dear?
Libby (*turning it into a cough*) Just a tickle. I'd better be off then.
Claire Yes. (*To Derek*) She's got "Thingy's" meal to get.
Derek Whose meal?
Claire There, she's got me at it. Tony's.
Libby Yes, must go. (*Confidentially to Derek*) Hope it works out.
Claire What works out?
Libby Must go. Bye.

Libby exits UL

Claire She gets battier.
Derek Well, she doesn't get it from me.

There's a crash from upstairs

Claire Shush! There's someone upstairs. (*Pushing Derek towards the hall*) Quick, get a golf-club from the hall cupboard!
Derek It's only the lodger.
Claire Make sure it's an iron! What?
Derek Our new lodger. Moved in this afternoon.
Claire Moved in! You promised ——
Derek Offered me a hundred and fifty quid.
Claire For a week? Not full board?
Derek No extras, he said.
Claire Wow ... (*Crossing towards the kitchen*) Didn't I say it was a good idea?

Claire exits to the kitchen

Derek But I think we should offer him a meal just this once. So we can get to know each other.
Claire (*off*) All right, just this once; as long as he doesn't get the wrong idea. Hell!
Derek (*calling to her*) What's up?
Claire (*off*) I've left the herbs Zoe gave me on her kitchen table.
Derek Well, we'll have to do without. She's gone into town.

Claire returns with knives and forks, etc.

Claire No, it's all right, we've got a key. (*Pointedly*) It's on the keyboard in the kitchen, marked Z for Zoe. I'm sure she won't mind. (*She pauses, waiting for Derek's offer which doesn't come*) I'll go.

The Upstairs Cuckoo

Derek No, you lay the table. I'll go.

Derek goes off UL

Claire (*calling after him*) What if "Thingy" comes down!

Derek pops his head round the door

Derek It's Steve, actually. Make yourself known to him.

Derek goes

Claire Oh God, not another Steve! I'm cursed with that name.

She starts to lay the table

Steve enters down the stairs and stands looking at her

She is unaware of him for a few moments. He coughs. She turns, sees him and screams

Steve (*rushing to her, grabbing her wrists and pinning her against the stairs*) Don't scream! Just listen a moment!
Claire (*struggling*) Let go of me, you swine!
Steve I only have your interests at heart.
Claire (*trying to fight him off*) Liar!
Steve Listen for one minute, then I'll go.

Claire stops her struggling, Steve lets her go

Claire All right, you have thirty seconds then I'll start screaming again.
Steve (*leading her* DC) You don't love old Dirk. I'm your man. You need me and I need you.

Claire tries to hit him but he grabs her arms

Claire You're beyond belief! I need you like Nelson Mandela needs apartheid.
Steve Listen! I'll make a bargain. Let me stay for a month and — if you want it — I'll give you a divorce.

Claire stops struggling again

Claire On what grounds?
Steve (*letting her go*) I'll confess, quite untruthfully, to adultery.
Claire Why are you doing this, Steve?
Steve Because I love you and I know you love me, even if you don't realize it.
Claire (*with vehemance, moving* DR) I don't!
Steve (*coming to her*) And a month, seeing us side by side, will convince you of your mistake.
Claire (*sitting in the* DR *chair*) Let me see if I've got this right: you're saying that if you live here for a month as the lodger, I shall be so impressed with seeing "Superman" — that's you, by the way — contrasted with poor little Derek that I shall come over all wobbly and realize what a silly girl I've been.
Steve (*moving to her*) Right.
Claire (*jumping up*) God, I always knew you were conceited but this takes the biscuit. (*Turning back to him*) You're on. One month from now, out you go straight to the solicitors and start divorce proceedings. Agreed?
Steve (*taking her in his arms*) Agreed, my darling.
Claire (*freeing herself*) And in the meantime, you'll behave like the perfect lodger.
Derek (*off, from the kitchen*) Claire, this stew's more than ready. Do you want me to add the herbs?
Claire (*calling*) No, I'm just coming. (*To Steve*) What shall I call you? Mr what?

The Upstairs Cuckoo

Steve Er — how about Noble?
Claire Noble?
Steve Mr Noble. Why not?
Claire (*collecting the* L *chair and placing it above the table*) Couldn't you have thought of something more appropriate, like Bustard?

Derek enters from the kitchen, carrying two cups of tea

Derek Fancy a cup of tea, Steve? I've just made one by mistake. Thought it was early morning.
Steve Thanks very much. Nice to be waited on for a change.
Derek Oh, sorry. Have you two introduced yourselves?
Claire Yes. Would you believe he's called Steve Noble?
Steve Sometimes, Noble Steve.
Claire (*spluttering*) Good God!
Derek No offence, old man, it's just that her ex was called Steve. She has an aversion to the name.
Claire And to its owner.
Derek He was the pits.
Steve Was? Is he dead?
Claire (*grimly*) Not yet.
Derek No, she had to leave him. The man was impossible.
Claire Quite impossible.
Derek So, you see, "Steve" is not the name of the month.
Steve What a shame. Well, never mind, you can always use my second name: Caesar.
Claire (*sarcastically*) Not "I came, I saw, I conquered" Caesar?
Steve He did, didn't he?
Claire I'll manage with "Steve".
Derek I can see you two are going to get on like a house on fire. You will have dinner with us tonight, won't you, Steve? I'm sure Claire would be delighted, wouldn't you, darling?

Claire (*sarcastically*) Over the moon.
Derek How about it, Steve? Just for your first night? Can't make it full board with Claire working, I'm afraid, but it would be nice to break the ice.
Steve Delighted. And don't worry about not being able to offer full board. I'm quite happy with bed and breakfast or just bed if it comes to that.
Claire It won't come to that. I can assure you. (*Going to the kitchen*) I'll serve up then.

Claire exits to the kitchen

Derek Only one of Claire's stews, I'm afraid.
Steve Oh my God!
Derek I beg your pardon?
Steve Oh my God, how I love stew.
Derek Oh, well, I hope you won't be disappointed, cooking's not Claire's forte.
Steve Too true.
Derek What?
Steve I shan't be disappointed.
Derek Oh.
Claire (*off, from the kitchen*) Give me a hand, Derek!
Derek Oh, right. (*Going to the kitchen*) Er, sit down, Steve, old chap. Make yourself at home.

Derek exits

Steve I will, Derek, old friend. (*With self-satisfaction*) I will. (*He sits*)

Claire and Derek enter from the kitchen. Derek carries three plates and Claire has a crockpot of stew which she places on

The Upstairs Cuckoo

the table so that Derek cannot put the plates down. He dances about, blowing on his fingers, until Claire makes a space for the plates

Derek (*putting down the plates hurriedly*) Phew, they were hot!
Claire (*putting down the crockpot*) Do you like goulash, Mr Noble?
Steve Oh, call me Steve, please.
Claire I don't know which is worse.
Derek (*hurriedly*) She means being starchy by using your surname or using the dreaded appellation "Steve". (*Sitting; under his breath to Claire*) What's the matter with you?
Claire (*under her breath to Derek*) Nothing! (*Serving out the goulash*) I hope this will be all right. It was a recipe in my crockpot book but I thought it might be a bit dull so I've livened it up with a few extra herbs.

Steve groans. Derek and Claire stare at him

Steve (*hurriedly*) I'm sure it will be delicious to me. I've had nothing but canteen food since I lost my wife.
Claire Oh, you mislaid her, did you?
Derek Claire! Steve and his wife have split up. It's a very painful subject for him.
Claire Yes, of course it is. Sorry, Steve. I expect you miss her dreadfully?
Steve If only she were here now.
Claire You miss her cooking, I expect.
Steve No, that's the only silver lining. She's the world's worst cook.
Claire Is she really? It's a good job she's not around to hear you say that becuase if she was your sweet would be laced with strychnine.

She sits and they eat in silence

Derek What makes a woman leave a man, I wonder?
Claire Criticizing her cooking perhaps.
Derek Mind you, when you get a swine like Claire's ex. I mean, it's a wonder she stayed with him the duration of the honeymoon.
Steve Rotten, was he?
Claire As a fallen apple. But I'm sure I don't know why we're talking about him. He's of no consequence now.
Derek Right, let's change the subject. You into computers, Steve?
Steve Not exactly. I've dabbled, of course, but engineering's really my line.
Claire Oh God, not engineering!
Derek (*under his breath to Steve*) He's an engineer.
Claire I thought we weren't going to talk about him.
Steve Seems a difficult man to keep at bay. Keeps popping up, doesn't he?
Claire So did Dracula.
Derek Actually we rarely mention him. The past is the past, that's what I always say.
Claire And should be left in the past.
Derek Right, what have we got for sweet?
Claire Apple pie.
Steve Oh no, not apple pie.
Claire (*icily*) And what's wrong with it?
Steve Sorry.
Derek I should think so too. Claire's good enough to offer you a meal. She didn't have to, you know.
Steve No, I'm sorry. It's just that I have a particular aversion to apple pie. It was an automatic response. Didn't mean to be rude or ungrateful.

Claire You could have fooled me.
Derek All right, darling, he has apologized.
Claire Uh!
Derek He may have good reason for avoiding apple pie. It could upset him.
Steve You see, my wife was always making apple pies and well ——
Claire (*ominously*) Yes?
Steve Well, to be perfectly honest, she couldn't make pastry to save her life.
Claire Really? I hope you told her that.
Steve No, never did. Couldn't bring myself to hurt her feelings.
Claire (*gathering up the dishes*) Right, no apple pie for you!
Steve I say, I hope I haven't offended. I'm sure your pies are delicious.
Derek Of course they are. You shouldn't take these remarks personally, darling. He's referring to his wife, not to you.
Claire Of course. Sorry if I'm a little confused. (*With great self-control*) I can offer you some cheese instead.
Steve Lovely.
Claire (*going to the kitchen*) My speciality, cutting cheese.

Claire exits

The front doorbell rings

Derek All right, I'll get it.

Derek exits to the hall and there is the sound of the front door opening

(*Off*) Oh, it's only you!

Libby enters, followed by Derek

Libby (*entering*) Yes, it's only me. (*Going to the kitchen*) Sorry, forgot my back-door key. I dashed off and left Thingy's dinner in your fridge.

Derek In our fridge?

Libby turns back to him

Steve Hello again, Libby. It is Libby, isn't it?

Libby Give over, Da — Dashing, Mr er ——

Steve Noble.

Libby (*with a shriek of laughter*) Noble! (*To Derek*) Yes, Mum said I could have the cold beef from yesterday.

Derek Lucky old Thingy. (*Going to the kitchen*) I'd better get it. Your mother's a little fraught at the moment.

Derek exits

Libby Dad, what have you been saying?

Steve Nothing, nothing at all. I think it's because she realizes what a mistake she's made.

Libby In letting you stay, you mean?

Steve No, certainly not. In leaving me. She knows how I love her.

Libby How does she? When did you last tell her?

Steve I shouldn't need to tell her. It should be obvious.

Libby By the way you ignore her, you mean.

Steve Look, I may not be good at showing my feelings but she should know.

Libby (*going to him, sitting on his knee and stroking his hair*) Poor, old Daddy, what a mass of inhibitions you are. If only you could stop playing macho man and be yourself, your real cuddly self.

She puts her arms round his neck and he responds by enfolding her in his

The Upstairs Cuckoo

Derek enters carrying a plastic bag in which is the cold meat

Derek There's not all that much —— (*He stops on seeing Libby*)

Libby jumps up and turns away. Derek goes to her, grabs her arm and throws her into the armchair R

    Good God, girl, have you no standards at all?
Steve (*rising*) Now look here!
Derek No, you look here and get out of this house at once!
Libby (*rising*) Derek, you don't understand ——
Derek No, I don't but I know what I see. (*Pushing her down again*) Hussy!
Steve (*grabbing Derek*) Take that back!

Claire runs in

Derek knocks Steve to the ground

Derek Bloody pervert!
Claire (*rushing to the prostrate Steve and cradling his head*) Steve! Steve! Speak to me, my darling. (*To Derek*) Beast! (*To Steve*) I didn't mean all those things I said. You are my first and only love. (*To Derek*) Get a doctor!
Derek When you've quite finished throwing yourself at a complete stranger, he's not hurt.
Claire Of course he's hurt, you monster you!
Derek He's feigning.
Claire He's not! (*To Steve*) Are you?
Steve (*pretending to come to*) Where am I?
Claire (*hitting him*) He is! He bloody is! (*Jumping to her feet*) I hate him!
Derek I prefer that.

Claire And you!

She pushes Steve to the floor again

I hate all men! (*Moving rapidly to the front door*) Come on, Libby, let's go to a nunnery.

Claire exits

Libby follows, moving between Derek and Steve, pushing Steve to the floor again

Libby I don't know about that but I'm off men.
Derek (*holding up the plastic bag*) Don't forget Thingy's dinner.
Libby Thingy can get his own dinner.

Libby exits

Steve (*clambering to his feet*) I'm sorry, Derek old boy. I'm afraid I've messed things up for the both of us.
Derek I imagine you must be ——
Steve The absolute swine, the rotten apple — yes.
Derek Well, you're not a bit like Claire painted you, I must say. In fact, even though we've been rivals, I'd call you a nice guy.
Steve Well thanks, Derek. I must say you're not a bit like I imagined. I had you down as a wimp, nanny substitute, you know. Interested in ballet and cooking but (*feeling his jaw*) you're a man after my own heart.
Derek Well, I do like ballet and I'm a tolerable cook.
Steve Of course, you need to be with Claire. I say, ever thought of sharing a flat?
Derek People would talk.
Steve Of course but what wonderful cover: we'd be trusted alone with any female.

Derek And we could keep the costs to a minimum.

They shake hands

Steve No more female inconsistencies.
Derek No more female extravagances.
Steve }
Derek } (*together*) No more apple pie!

CURTAIN

FURNITURE AND PROPERTY LIST

On stage: Table. *On it*: telephone
Coffee-table
Two easy chairs
Dining-table. *On it*: folded cloth
Three dining-chairs

Off stage: Bottle of sherry, two glasses (**Claire**)
Large suitcase (**Derek**)
Small suitcase (**Steve**)
Three sets of knives and forks (**Claire**)
Two cups of tea (**Derek**)
Three dinner plates (**Derek**)
Crockpot of stew, serving ladle (**Claire**)
Cold meat in plastic bag (**Derek**)

LIGHTING PLOT

Property fittings required: nil.

Interior. The same scene throughout.

To open: Full, general lighting

No cues

EFFECTS PLOT

Cue 1	**Derek** exits to the kitchen *Telephone*	(Page 6)
Cue 2	**Derek** puts the phone down *Doorbell*	(Page 6)
Cue 3	**Derek:** "... get it from me." *Crash from upstairs*	(Page 14)
Cue 4	**Claire** exits *Doorbell*	(Page 21)

www.ingramcontent.com/pod-product-compliance
Ingram Content Group UK Ltd.
Pitfield, Milton Keynes, MK11 3LW, UK
UKHW021842140426
5217IPUK00022B/1557